To My Moose Friends

A Book of Moosery Rhymes

Christina Simpson
&
Benjamin Partlow

*To Reece, Happy Searching!
Christina Simpson*

To My Moose Friends: A Book of Moosery Rhymes
By Christina Simpson and Benjamin Partlow

Published by Moose Print Publishing

Copyright ©2021 Christina Simpson and Benjamin Partlow

All rights reserved. No portion of this book may be reproduced in any form without permission from the publisher, except as permitted by U.S. copyright law.

Cover photograph by Thomas Drasdauskis, Bowron Recreation

ISBN: 978-0-578-96283-2 (print)

To My Moose Friends
To the tune of "Twinkle Twinkle Little Star"

To my moose friends near and far,
How I wonder where you are.
Climb a mountain, eat a tree,
Then won't you come play with me?
To my moose friends near and far,
Won't you tell me where you are?

To my moose friends near and far,
How I wonder where you are.
In the woodlands, in the marsh,
Leaving droppings, eating bark.
To my moose friends near and far,
Won't you tell me where you are?

♠ DID YOU KNOW?

Moose must consume almost 10,000 calories (or up to 70 lbs) of food per day to maintain their body weight.

The Long-Legged Moose

To the tune of "The Itsy Bitsy Spider"

The long-legged brown-haired moose
climbed up the mountaintop.

Along came the hikers
with their mom and pop.

The long-legged brown-haired moose
stood proudly for all to see,

And the hikers came back down
to tell their tale to you and me.

DID YOU KNOW?

Moose are the largest member of the deer family, standing up to 7 ft at the shoulder and weighing 1800 lbs.

Big Antlers
To the tune of "Mary Had a Little Lamb"

The moose he had such big antlers, big antlers, big antlers.
The moose he had such big antlers,
To defend his friends from foes.

In the fall he loses them, loses them, loses them.
In the fall he loses them,
Before the winter snows.

In the spring they grow again, grow again, grow again.
In the spring they grow again,
The cycle goes and goes.

All Around the Hobble-y Bush

To the tune of "Pop! Goes the Weasel"

All around the hobble-y bush,

The moose, they eat the buds.

The buds, they make them big and strong,

To STOMP through the woods.

All around the balsam boughs,

The moose, they eat the needles.

The needles make them big and strong,

To PRANCE through the fields.

🫎 DID YOU KNOW?

The name "moose" comes from the Native American word "moswa," which translates to "twig-eater."

I'm a Little Moosey

To the tune of "I'm a Little Teapot"

I'm a little moosey, tall and grand.
Here are my antlers, where I stand.
When you try to find me, watch me hide.
Look for tracks, they'll be your guide.

I'm a little moosey, where'd I go?
Find my hoofprints, deep in the snow.
When you try to find me, hear my call.
I'll be nearby, standing tall.

DID YOU KNOW?

Male moose have up to a 52 sq mi home range.

Moose Friend

To the tune of "Baa Baa Black Sheep"

Moose friend, moose friend, do you have a calf?
Yes sir, yes sir, two and a half.
One's all grown up now,
One's out to play.
One isn't here yet, she's still on the way.
Moose friend, moose friend, do you have a calf?
Yes sir, yes sir, two and a half.

DID YOU KNOW?

Moose calves weigh about 35 lbs at birth and can gain 2.2 lbs per day while nursing.

M-O-O-S-E

To the tune of "Bingo"

There was a hiker in the woods,

A moose she wanted to see -

M-O-O-S-E

M-O-O-S-E

M-O-O-S-E

A moose she wanted to see!

The Legs on the Moose

To the tune of "The Wheels on the Bus"

The legs on the moose go tromp tromp tromp,

Tromp tromp tromp,

Tromp tromp tromp.

The legs on the moose go tromp tromp tromp,

All through the woods.

The mouth on the moose goes chomp chomp chomp,

Chomp chomp chomp,

Chomp chomp chomp.

The mouth on the moose goes chomp chomp chomp,

All through the woods.

The nose on the moose goes sniff sniff sniff,
Sniff sniff sniff,
Sniff sniff sniff.
The nose on the moose goes sniff sniff sniff,
All through the woods.

The antlers on the moose go left right left,
Left right left,
Left right left.
The antlers on the moose go left right left,
All through the woods.

The tail on the moose goes waggle waggle waggle,

Waggle waggle waggle,

Waggle waggle waggle.

The tail on the moose goes waggle waggle waggle,

All through the woods.

The fur on the moose goes brrrrrrrrrrrrrrrr!

Brrrrrrrrrrrrrrrr!

Brrrrrrrrrrrrrrrr!

The fur on the moose goes brrrrrrrrrrrrrrrr!

All through the snow.

🫎 DID YOU KNOW?

The flap under the moose's chin is called a "dewlap."

Happy Searching!

CPSIA information can be obtained
at www.ICGtesting.com
Printed in the USA
LVHW071100161221
706124LV00002B/15

About the Authors

Benjamin Partlow grew up in Ludlow, Vermont and loved animals from an early age. He spent much of his childhood exploring the woods behind his house and trying to find moose, deer, bear, and more.

Christina Simpson grew up in neighboring Massachusetts and saw her first moose on a trip to Maine. She quickly developed an appreciation for these majestic animals, especially as Ben started pointing out all the signs they left behind in the woods.

Together they composed these nursery rhymes while hiking the 4000 footers across New England.